THE
ASKING
FORMULA

ASK FOR WHAT YOU WANT...AND GET IT!

JOHN BAKER

Wonsockon Publishers Minneapolis, MN

© 2012 John Baker

Published by
Wonsockon Publishers
Minneapolis, MN

Publisher's Cataloging-in-Publication Data
Baker, John

The Asking Formula : ask for what you want- and get it! / John Baker. – Minneapolis, MN : Wonsockon Publishers, 2012.

p. ; cm.

ISBN13: 978-0-9818852-3-0

1. Sales meetings. 2. Sales management. 3. Business communication. I. Title.

HF5438.8.M4 B35 2012
658.8101—dc23   2012944854

FIRST EDITION

Project coordination by Jenkins Group, Inc.
www.BookPublishing.com

Cover and interior art by Janelle B., Studio 7 Design Inc.
Interior design by Brooke Camfield

Printed in the United States of America
16   15   14   13   12   •   5   4   3   2   1

For Tammy. I asked and you said yes.

Warren is a quiet man, small in stature, quick with a smile, and as dependable as the tides. Twice a year he comes to my house and washes all my windows.

I love him for this.

I love him for this because my house has a lot of windows. I love him for this because I hate washing windows. I love him for this because I washed my house's windows once, and when I think back on that experience, I love him even more.

The day had not started out to be a great one, so it was an especially welcome sight to see Warren pull up in his white van—complete with a squeegee hood ornament and emboldened with the words "Warren the Window Washer" written in bright red. On the side was a decal of a smiling sponge on steroids and the caption "Top to Bottom. Inside and Out. Windows, Sills, and Screens."

I had brought a lot of work home. Again. I had promised my twelve-year-old daughter that I would go around the neighborhood with her selling candy door-to-door for her soccer team. My son was moping about and suffering from some new strain of teenage malaise. And, my wife, Gracie—who is a wizard dealing with this type of adolescent melancholy—was away at a ladies' golf weekend.

The day was sunny and bright, and the weather promised to hold through the weekend. This was good news for Gracie but made me even gloomier as I looked at the pile of work—precariously tilting like the Tower of Pisa—stacked in front of me.

But what had really put me in a surly mood was that the week had ended with the depressing news that my company was going to lose the McNeal Hotels bid, a prospect we had spent nearly four months and tens of thousands of dollars courting.

When Warren arrived, I was holding court with a pot of coffee out on my front patio and thinking dark thoughts. He greeted me with a nod and started to set up his ladder, fill his buckets, and arrange his window-cleaning supplies.

"Good to see you, Warren. How's business?" I asked him, half out of courtesy and half as a strategy to avoid the work in front of me.

"I'm really cleaning up," Warren said with a grin while holding up his sponge and squeezing soapy water back into the bucket. "Cleaning up," he repeated in case I didn't get the joke the first time. "Business could not be better."

"Can I offer you a cup of coffee?" I asked.

"Already had my coffee this morning," he replied with a shake of his head. "And, I have a full slate of clients to get to today, so I'll pass. But I appreciate the offer."

I sat drinking my coffee and watched the chickadees eat at my feeder. It occurred to me that it had been a long time since I had heard anyone say that he or she had a "full slate of clients" and that "business couldn't be better."

My business certainly could be better, and I thought again about the lost McNeal Hotels account, like a nagging toothache. It had been only the most recent of a series of setbacks. Fact was my division was struggling. I would have liked to chalk it up to a tough market or the bad economy, but, in truth, our competition was beating us. Even with solid products and a veteran staff, I was finding it hard to close business and generate new sales.

Apparently this was not Warren's problem.

"Business could not be better," he had said, and for all I knew that was probably true. I certainly saw his truck all over the neighborhood. His business couldn't be any more different from mine—I sold complex products to big corporations, and he sold window washing to individual homeowners—but running a successful business is tough no matter what.

"What's your secret, Warren? How come your business is so good?"

He was already halfway up the ladder, but he stopped and looked down at me.

"Windows get dirty and need washing," he said, shrugging. "I work top to bottom, inside and out, and I do the windows, sills, and screens."

He smiled and started back up the ladder.

"Well, you're good at what you do," I said. "Business must be falling in your lap."

"Wish it were true," he replied nonchalantly from above. "But that's not the case. No matter how good you are, you have to know how to ask for what you want. Something that took me a spell to learn."

He hooked his bucket to the top rung of the ladder, plunged his sponge into the sudsy contents, and slathered just the right amount of soapy water over the windowpane.

I watched him work and admired his effortless routine: plunge, apply, squeegee, and wipe. Repeat. It was mesmerizing.

He'd start at the upper panes of the window and work down to the lower ones. Thin fingers of water would stream down and pool on the window's sill. Warren used this soapy residue to wipe the sill clean with a quick and effortless pass of his rag.

The graceful fluidity of his work was like watching a master chef dice an onion: impressive and mundane all at the same time. I looked at the overflowing stack of budget statements, sales presentations, spreadsheets, reports, and staffing requests on my patio table and thought: there is nothing graceful in all of that.

In a matter of minutes, Warren finished the window he was working on and descended to reposition his ladder to reach the next window.

"Warren," I asked, "what did you mean when you said it took you a while to learn how to ask for what you want?"

He leaned his foot on the first rung of the ladder. He set his bucket on the ground and wiped his hands dry on a towel hanging from his belt. He thought to himself for a minute.

"It was tough starting out," he finally said. "There was a lot of competition. Still is. Anybody with a bucket and a sponge qualifies as a window washer. I was new and unknown. A lot of folks stick with the company that cleaned their windows the year before. I wasn't very successful until I learned how to ask for what I wanted."

"I can relate," I said. "Same story in my business. It's a battle out there, and it's getting tougher. It's really hard to get new clients. What did you do to break in?"

"I tried a lot of things," Warren replied. "I cut my prices, figuring it might generate some interest—and it did . . . some. But, cutting prices backfired since all I did for that first year was talk about how cheap I was."

He looped his towel back around his belt.

"I thought I could win business by marketing my window washing as better than the next guy's, but most people figure washing a window isn't rocket science—and they'd be right about that. Frankly, it's hard to tell the difference between what I do from what the next guy does," he said with a big shrug of his shoulders.

I sipped my coffee and marveled that even an unpretentious window washer worried about differentiating his service from that of his competition. My team had spent countless hours trying to differentiate ourselves in the McNeal Hotels bid. *A lot of good that did.* We presented a list of FABs (features, advantages, and benefits) that would have choked a Clydesdale. "The more, the better" was our motto. "Leave nothing in the quiver." But, in the end, the McNeal people decided to pass on our proposal and go with the competitor's offering. It stung: all that hard work for nothing. Closing the McNeal Hotels account would have made the year. It would have turned our momentum around. I felt I had let my team down.

Warren started talking again and interrupted my thoughts.

"I offered package deals," he continued. "Got bonded. Mailed coupons. Heck, I even had one of the boys set me up on Facebook. And, all of it won an occasional client. But nothing produced consistent results until I learned about the Asking Formula."

I waited for Warren to finish his thought, but apparently he had.

He started up the ladder again, but before he had gone too far, I asked, "What's the Asking Formula?"

He scaled back down to the ground, leaned back on his heels a little, and took a good look at me. Finally, as if convincing himself of something, he submerged his finger into the soapy water in his cleaning bucket and wrote this on the dirty window next to my patio table:

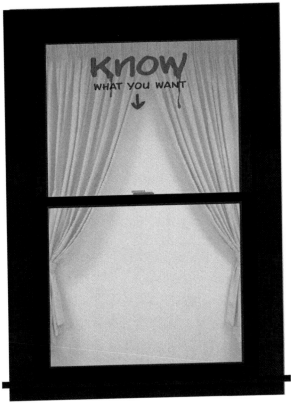

I looked at the window as if it were one of those stereogram prints that if stared at long enough turns into a 3-D Elvis. I looked back at Warren. Was he trying to put one over on me? A prank at my expense? A "stupid client" story he'd yuck up with the boys at the next window washer convention?

"That's not much of a formula," I said skeptically. "It's pretty simple."

Warren stood akimbo and looked at his writing like it was a Picasso.

"Simple but it'll change your life," he replied. "Most people don't take the time to know what they want before asking for what they want, which generally means they don't get what they want."

Was this a joke?

But Warren didn't look like he was joking.

Know what you want.

Hmm.

I thought about the number of dead-end sales calls I participated in where nothing was settled and nothing was gained.

I thought of the endless meetings I attended in airless rooms with rock-hard seats that concluded with me asking myself, What is it these people want me to do?

I thought about the number of phone calls, text messages, e-mails, and voicemails I received each and every day. My typical reaction: So what? What does this have to do with me? Why is this my problem?

Based simply on a normal day's sampling, I had to conclude that I was surrounded by people who did not know what they wanted.

Warren was squeezing excess water off his sponge into the bucket.

"I'll grant you have a point, Warren," I said, "but it seems kind of . . . well, obvious."

"It *is* obvious," Warren answered with a snort. "Which is why it's so strange that people don't take the time to know what they want before they ask for it."

I held my hands up in confusion.

"But, doesn't everyone 'know what they want'?" I asked.

"Not by a long shot. I'll give you an example," Warren said. "I was shopping for a new computer last week for the business. This won't come as a big surprise to you, but I'm a guy who likes to keep things simple, and I was looking for something to handle basic billing and accounting tasks. Nothing fancy. I was asking this young fella some questions about this particular computer that was on sale. He sure knew his stuff. He went on and on about these features this particular computer had to offer. He seemed really enthralled with the thing. I came away from that conversation thinking he was a very bright young man. But, I didn't buy a computer from him."

"He didn't have what you needed?" I asked.

"I don't know," Warren observed wryly. "If he wanted me to know that he was really smart, then he accomplished his goal. If he wanted to convince me that he had memorized the sales literature, he was very convincing. But, if he wanted to sell me a computer, he missed the boat entirely."

The coffee in my cup had turned cold, and I tossed the brown liquid out on the lawn. I refilled my cup and took a sip. I couldn't help but relive the McNeal Hotels account in my brain. We had been masterful in presenting our product and services. There wasn't one question we hadn't been prepared to answer. I was convinced that the people at McNeal were convinced that *we were convinced* we knew what we were talking about. But, I was beginning to sense that we had significantly missed something in our planning.

I wondered whether we knew what we wanted with McNeal. Our presentation hadn't been tethered to any one thing. It meandered two and a half hours—well over the allotted time—zigging to this topic and zagging to that. It was as if we weren't hitched to anything specific.

I looked at Warren's handiwork on the window: if we didn't know what we wanted, how did we expect McNeal to know?

As if to break the spell, Warren said, "Not knowing what you want before asking for what you want means not getting what you want. The first step in the Asking Formula is 'Know what you want.'"

"OK," I nodded grudgingly, "but there has to be more to the formula than that."

He smiled and said, "Oh, there is."

He resubmerged his finger into the soapy water and went back to the patio window and wrote:

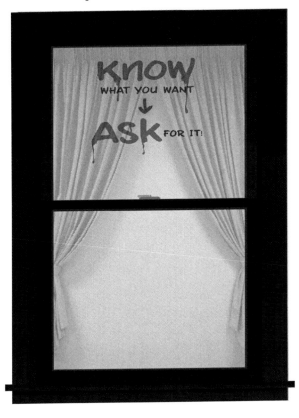

"Ask . . . for . . . it?" I sounded out the words as if reading from an elementary school English primer.

"Yes," said Warren. "Step two of the Asking Formula is to ask for what you want."

"Immediately?" I reacted, taken aback. I shook my head. "No, that doesn't sound right. It seems too direct, almost rude, to ask for what you want right up front. Shouldn't there be an interim period or some type of 'priming of the pump' that goes on before you get right to asking? I typically try to soften the audience up a little before I go in for the kill."

"Actually, that's the worst thing you can do," said Warren. "Being vague about asking for what you want makes your audience guess at what you want. Usually, that doesn't turn out so well."

Warren paused for a moment and then with a straight face said, "I guess what happens in vagueness stays in vagueness." Then, in case I didn't get the joke, he said, "You know, like they say in those Las Vegas commercials?"

"Very funny," I grimaced. "But, I don't think it's overly common for people to be that direct asking somebody for something they want."

"Well, there you go," Warren said with a small nod as if I had just made his point for him. "How many of the good things in your life have you gotten that you didn't ask for?"

Now that's a good question, I thought.

"Not too many, I guess," I said. I shook my head and laughed at the very absurdity of the notion. "In fact, I try to teach my kids that if there is one thing in this world I have learned, it's that you have to speak up for yourself to get the things you want in life. No one is going to give you a free pass. Good things aren't just handed out on a silver platter."

"Good things are not just handed out," Warren agreed. "You have to ask for them. That's what's behind step two of the Asking Formula. Not asking means not getting. Asking is the most important skill for getting what you want."

I thought about the quote from Wayne Gretzky, one of my favorite pro athletes and arguably the best person to ever play hockey, who said, "You miss 100% of the shots you don't take." Not asking means getting a "no" 100% of the time. If you don't ask, you don't get.

"All right, Warren, I'll concede that this formula of yours works in certain situations, but I'm not so sure it would work very well in a business environment. Asking for what you want right away isn't the way things get done. It's too abrupt. There's this whole philosophy of 'consultative selling' that says we should thoroughly understand our prospects' concerns before trying to sell them anything."

"Well, I don't know about that," said Warren. "I like to keep things simple, and it seems to me that most people like the direct approach. They don't have enough time in their day to get things done as it is. That's why they bring work home and hire someone like me to do their windows."

Warren saw me wince as I glanced at my pile of work.

"Sorry, I didn't mean anything personal by that," he said. "But my guess is that certain people get so tied up in the . . . what did you call it . . . the 'consultative' part of a conversation that they forget to get to the point. Eventually, to get what you want, you've got to ask for it."

I froze with my cup halfway up to my lips. A lightbulb— no, make that a 5,000-watt Klieg light—went on in my brain. "Eureka," I almost shouted. Without knowing it, Warren had just described some members of my sales team to a tee. They used conversation as a crutch to avoid having to ask for the sale. Instead of getting to the point, they procrastinated and avoided pressing for what they wanted. They justified their reluctance by saying they needed more information or hid their actions under the cloak of being sociable with their clients.

But a big part of what they were doing was avoiding asking for what they wanted.

I realized how common this bad habit was. Directness is a rare thing these days. As a matter of fact, when someone

asks directly for what he or she wants, it's so uncommon—
and refreshing—that it sets that person apart.

I was really enjoying my conversation with Warren,
but I could see that he was eager to get back to his work. I
had to get to my work as well.

"Were you always good at being this upfront about
asking for what you want?" I asked.

"Fact is," said Warren, wringing his hands on his
towel, "at first I rarely asked for what I wanted."

"How's that?" I asked, surprised.

Warren shrugged. "Didn't want to get no for an
answer, I suppose. And, that's a pretty sure way to starve.
Because if you're not willing to ask and get a 'no,' you're
not going to get a 'yes,' either."

Warren took off his cap and scratched his head. "I
told people all the reasons they should hire me, and some-
where in all that jibber-jabbering, I tried to ask for what
I wanted without actually asking for it. That doesn't work
so well. Of course, that was before I learned the Asking
Formula."

I sipped some coffee and thought about what he said.

"So," I said, "your business took off when you started
asking—directly asking—for what you wanted instead
of giving all the reasons why you thought you should be
given what you wanted?"

"Exactly," Warren replied. "I ask for what I want. Like I said before, I like to keep things simple, and getting what I want is as simple as saying, 'I am asking you to hire me to wash your windows.'"

"And that's been the key to your success?"

"It's gotten me a considerable part of the way there," Warren said, "but there are other parts to the Asking Formula I had to learn."

Just then, my eldest son, Zack, came out of the house and joined me on the patio. Zack was a high school junior and having an even worse week than I was: a sixteen-year-old boy with girl trouble.

"Hello, Zack," Warren said. He excused himself and climbed back up the ladder.

"Hi, Warren," Zack called up after him. He folded his body like an accordion into a patio chair. He let out a big sigh.

"You OK?" I asked.

"It's Elizabeth," he said, throwing his arms into the air. "I've texted her three times this morning, and she hasn't texted back."

Elizabeth. Head cheerleader. Popular. Attractive. Zack's current infatuation.

"What are you texting her about?" I asked.

"I want to ask her out next Friday," Zack said. "She won't return any of my messages."

"Well," I said, "you could try that new thingamajig called the telephone. I was talking to Grandpa, and he said that it's a pretty cool technology where you can speak to people and they actually hear your voice. Or, better yet, you could go over to her house, knock on her front door, and ask her out in person."

"Yeah, right, like that would work," Zack said, huffing and rolling his eyes. He launched himself off the chair and stormed back into the house.

I looked up at Warren, who was busy finishing a window. He came down to reposition his ladder.

"Girl troubles," I said, tilting my head toward Zack's retreating back.

"I've got three boys of my own," Warren said, nodding with understanding.

Before he got back on the ladder, I asked him, "You said there were other parts to the Asking Formula. What other parts?"

Warren nodded, like he knew I was going to ask the question. "It is always easier for people to understand what you want if you show them what you are asking for. Showing what you're asking for is step three of the Asking Formula."

Warren plunged his finger back into the water bucket, walked back over to the window, and wrote:

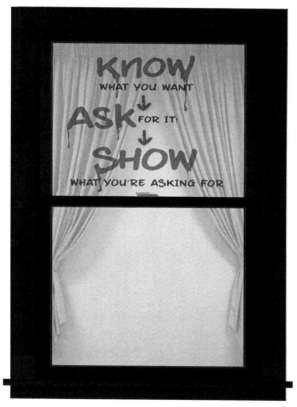

When he was done writing, he turned to me and asked, "Do you remember when you and I first met and I asked for your window-washing business?"

"It was a few years ago, Warren, and I have a seriously hard time remembering what I had to eat last night. But, I do recall that I was sitting right here on this patio when you walked up my driveway. You were hauling a big ladder on your shoulder and looked ready to dive right into the job."

"Actually, it was a small ladder—weighed about ten pounds," Warren replied. "I was also carrying a bucket filled with squeegees and sponges and the like."

"That's right. Now I remember," I said. "I recall thinking, This guy really wants my business. And, Gracie has wanted these windows washed for the past couple of weeks. But, before I can even start the job—which this guy can start right now—I'll need to get that damn rickety ladder of mine, find sponges (where I have not a clue) and a clean bucket (which I don't have), and go buy a squeegee. Then I'll have to get up on that damn rickety ladder and haul a bucket of water with me. Frankly, Warren, you had me at 'that damn rickety ladder.'"

Warren laughed. "That ladder was magic. I can't tell you how many jobs I won because of it. It was a pain to lug it around, but people could see *why they wanted to give me what I was asking for.* You didn't see me as someone to wash your windows; you saw me as someone who could help you avoid climbing up a damn rickety ladder."

I started to laugh along with him: "Ladders and me don't mix. That is true. So, Obi-Warren Kenobi, you played a Jedi mind trick on me."

He cracked a smile. "No, not really. I just know the first three steps of the Asking Formula: know what you want, ask for it, and show what you're asking for."

I sat back down at my table, and Warren climbed up the ladder once again.

Abby, my sparkling twelve-year-old daughter, came bounding around the corner of the house while hauling two cartons of candy each the size of a steamer trunk. As usual, she was overflowing with energy and enthusiasm.

"I'm ready for candy-selling duty, Dad. You ready to go?" she nearly shouted.

"No," I said, "I have no interest in mooching door-to-door. I'd rather climb up that ladder and help Warren wash windows. I'll just give you the money for all the candy. Now get something sugary to drink and go watch some TV while I sit here and have my coffee."

Which is not what I said. Rather: "Sure, I'm ready, Sweetheart. Let's go."

Abby started down the road, and I played the part of the pack mule and carried the two steamer trunks. The candy sales were to raise funds for the new soccer nets at the city park. Everyone on her team was expected to sell at least twenty-five boxes of candy. In the past month Abby had sold one box to her mother and one box to me. She had tried to sell one box to Zack, who huffed and rolled his eyes.

We made a loop up one side of Elm Street and down the other. Our method was for me to carry the candy, offer moral support, and help Abby keep track of money. Abby had to ring the doorbell at each house and do all the talking.

Several neighbors were either not at home or hiding behind their curtains. Our close neighbors, those we had gotten to know over the years, were all gracious enough to buy a box of candy from Abby. The neighbors we knew less well or didn't know at all were much more reluctant to buy and oftentimes surprisingly rude.

At each house I stood close enough to overhear Abby's pitch, which changed somewhat at each house but went something like this:

"Hi, I'm Abby, and I live down the street. I'm the goalkeeper on the Angels soccer team. To be part of the team and play in games, we have to sell candy to raise money. Would you like to buy some?"

It wasn't easy going door-to-door, and I was proud of Abby's better-late-than-never initiative. But, after several "noes," her resilience sagged. Most of the houses we visited turned her down even before she was done making her pitch. By the time we had made the loop around Elm Street and returned to our house, Abby was tired and dejected. She had sold only eight more boxes of candy.

I was really tempted to just buy the remaining boxes as I was first inclined but reckoned that fund-raising was part of Abby's responsibility of being an Angel, so I said, "Hey, Abby, let's take a break, get something to drink, and go over to Maple Street in a little while. We'll kill 'em over on Maple."

I poured us each some lemonade; she took hers to her room while I took mine outside to the patio table. I noticed that Warren was back up on the ladder and making rapid progress on the second-story windows.

As I drank my lemonade, I looked at what Warren had written on the patio window and reflected on our morning's conversation. The Asking Formula had made a lot of sense.

Warren interrupted my thoughts.

"How'd the candy selling go?" he asked from above.

"Ever see the movie *A Nightmare on Elm Street*?" I replied looking up at him. "Abby's pretty dejected. It's tough work for a young kid. She's resting up before we attack the innocents over on Maple."

"Did you let Abby in on the Asking Formula?" Warren asked.

I reacted with surprise. "You know, it never dawned on me." Only half seriously I added, "Do you think she's old enough to understand it?"

"Wish I had learned it earlier in life," Warren replied. "Did Abby ask for what she wanted first?"

I thought about this for a second. "No, she didn't," I admitted.

"Did she show what she was asking for in order to help people understand what she wanted?"

"No," I said.

"Hmm," Warren frowned. "Did she use Best Reasons?"

"Best Reasons?" I said. "I don't think we covered that in class this morning, Professor. What's a Best Reason?"

Once again Warren descended the ladder, soaked his finger in his water bucket, walked over to the patio window, and wrote:

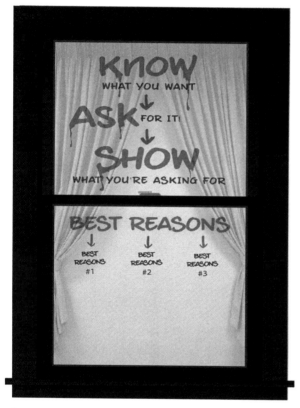

"Best Reasons are the reasons why someone would *want to give me what I am asking for*. It is the fourth step of the Asking Formula," he said.

"I don't know whether I follow you," I said.

Warren thought for a moment. "About the best way I can explain it is to think about a dirty window. Now, most folks don't decide their windows need washing by looking into their house from the outside. They see that their windows are dirty by looking out the window from the inside of the house. Same dirty pane of glass but two different views."

I nodded my head to let him know I was tracking—which I was . . . sort of.

"It's not much different with asking for what you want. It's what people see from their side of the glass that motivates them. It doesn't matter that I want to wash your windows because I see that they are dirty from the outside. If you don't care from your 'inside' view, then we won't be doing business. I have to get people to tell me their inside reasons: what's in it for them to have clean windows. These are the Best Reasons."

"How in the world do you do that?" I asked.

Warren shrugged nonchalantly and said, "There's no magic to it. Most people will gladly tell you if you ask."

"Warren," I said, "you might not remember this, but when you first sold me on your window-washing services, I recall that you walked up to me and declared, 'I bet I can guess—exactly—the number of windows you have in this house.' I remember saying to myself, 'Well, that's certainly an unusual icebreaker.' Since I had no idea how many windows the house has, I thought it would be quite some trick if some stranger actually could guess the number."

Warren threw his head back and laughed. "Of course, I remember. I told you that if I lost the bet, I'd throw a free car wash in as part of my service."

"And, if I recall," I said with mock smugness, "I got a free car wash out of the deal."

"And I got you as a client," Warren countered. "When we walked around the house and counted the windows, I asked you about the last time you had the windows cleaned. If you had any windows or screens that were damaged. If the screens had been washed recently. If you had any upcoming events you planned to host at your home. If you had a ladder big enough to reach that one window in the back that's over thirty feet from the ground."

"I get it," I said. "You were developing your Best Reasons."

"Exactly," Warren said. "Congratulations, you're really picking up on the Asking Formula."

"Well, thanks, Warren. It's different from anything else I've heard, but it's logical, and it makes a lot of sense."

Warren continued: "As we walked around the house, I began to really understand what was important to you. Not just clean windows but also the fact that you hated heights, and that your wife wanted the windows clean, and that you were planning a big Fourth of July party at your house, and that you liked to play golf whenever you could.

"Look here," said Warren, taking up a memo pad from my table. "Let me list all the reasons you gave me as to why you wanted to hire me to wash your windows."

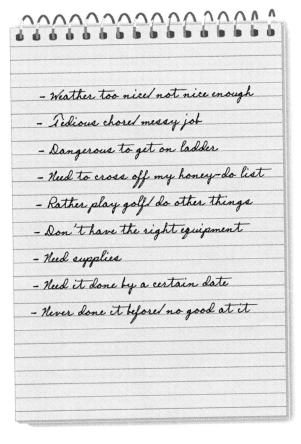

- Weather too nice/ not nice enough
- Tedious chore/ messy job
- Dangerous to get on ladder
- Need to cross off my honey-do list
- Rather play golf/ do other things
- Don't have the right equipment
- Need supplies
- Need it done by a certain date
- Never done it before/ no good at it

He handed me the list.

"Wow—you learned all of this in the time it took to walk around the house and count windows?" I asked in surprise. "And by the way, you have a great memory."

Warren smiled slightly. "To be honest," he said to me, "your reasons for wanting clean windows aren't all that much different from the next guy's. Like I said, window washing isn't rocket science."

"Even still, I'm impressed," I said.

"Don't be," Warren replied humbly. "The most important thing I did when we walked around the house was get you to talk about yourself and tell me what was important to you."

Warren paused. "Before learning the Asking Formula, I thought my job was to tell people why they should hire me to wash their windows," he continued. "Now I know that my job is to get them to tell me what's in it for them to have clean windows."

Wow, I thought to myself, that's quite a twist on the idea of selling.

"For example," Warren continued, "when you said that you were planning a big Fourth of July open house, I asked you how you would feel if everyone looked out at your wonderful landscaping through dirty windows. When I asked your thoughts about getting up on that ladder, I remember you told me that you're a little afraid of heights. And when you said that you would rather be golfing than spending time doing work, I asked whether you would rather play golf or clean windows. And you just laughed. I knew I had my three reasons."

He paused for a minute to see whether I had any questions. Then he continued: "The goal wasn't to sell you my window-washing service. The goal was to discover three reasons why you wanted me to wash your windows."

"Why three?" I asked.

"Who knows?" Warren shrugged. "It's just the way it is. We think in threes. ABC's, 1-2-3's, and do-re-mi's. Three blind mice, Goldilocks and the three bears, the three little pigs. Three Stooges, the Three Musketeers . . . You get the point. Real estate is all about—"

"Location, location, location," I interrupted.

"That's right," Warren said, grinning.

"But you've listed nine reasons why I would want to hire you to wash my windows," I observed.

"I knew nine was too many," Warren admitted. "So, I asked you questions that helped me whittle the list down to what your most important reasons were."

Warren took back the list and edited it as follows:

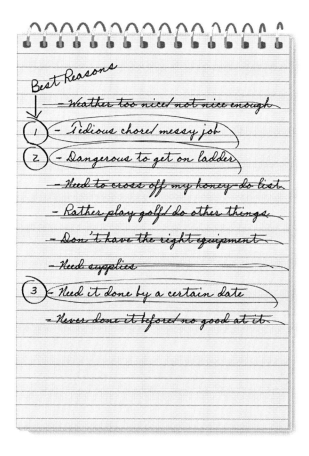

He gave the list back to me.

"The three Best Reasons why you wanted me to clean your windows," Warren said as he began counting off on his fingers:

"One, you wanted a quality job done but didn't want to take the time to do a tedious chore. Two, you didn't like the idea of climbing up on a ladder. And, three, you needed to have the job done by the open house you were hosting on the Fourth of July."

"I don't recall saying any of this," I stated.

"Keep in mind," Warren responded, "I was listening and you were talking."

I must have looked confused, because Warren said, "Is there something you don't understand?"

"No," I retorted, "this makes so much sense it's intuitive. I really like how straightforward it is. But, we discussed earlier that the problem with 'consultative selling' is that it can really extend the sales cycle and slows everything down. You put so much emphasis on asking questions I was wondering how you know when to stop asking questions."

"I like to keep things simple. Once I have three Best Reasons, I stop asking questions," Warren said.

Warren reached down and turned to another piece of paper in the tablet and drew this diagram:

Know what I want:
— Window-washing business

↓

Ask:
"I am asking you to hire me to wash your windows."

↓

Show: ladder + bucket

↓

Best Reasons

1. I'll do a quality job on a tough chore

2. You won't have to get up on this ladder

3. I'll have it done before the holiday weekend

I studied his diagram carefully. I could see how it flowed: from what Warren wanted, to what he asked for, to why I would want to give him what he was asking for.

I work top to bottom and inside and out, and I do windows, sills, and screens. That's what Warren had said when I asked earlier about the secret to his success. It was written on his van. Top to bottom. Inside out. Three Best Reasons.

"Looking at this," I observed, "it strikes me that the issue of price never came up. You got to my needs with your open-ended questioning. But, in my line of work some prospects care only about cost. What if they go right to price?"

"When people ask me about price, I immediately ask them two questions in return," Warren declared. "Honestly, why should I quote a price without knowing whether it's one of their Best Reasons?"

I really liked that answer. Just because someone asks about price doesn't automatically mean that you have to give him or her a quote. Maybe that's part of the first step in the Asking Formula. Once you know what you want, you're more willing to go after it and avoid getting sidetracked by questions on price or discounts.

"Warren, what happens next? Once you know your Best Reasons, what do you do?"

"Shut up."

"Excuse me?" I asked in surprise.

"Stop talking," Warren said with a wry smile. "It's time to listen for an answer. That's hard to do when you're still talking."

Warren walked up to the patio window and wrote:

Warren stepped back from the window.

"'Stop talking' is the fifth step of the Asking Formula," he said.

I realized that Warren had just written the antidote for the most common illness affecting salespeople: acute hyper-confabulation. We talk too much. We don't know when to zip it. We sell through the close. We don't give our audience a chance to answer.

"By the way, facts are important," Warren said. "Facts come in handy, but use them only if your listener wants more detail. Having your facts prepared, ready to go, and in your back pocket is step six of the Asking Formula."

He went to the window and with his wet finger wrote:

Reaching back for the notebook, Warren completed the Asking Formula diagram he had started.

"This is how an Asking Formula looks for my window-washing business: I know what I want. I ask for it. I show what I am asking for. I use three Best Reasons. And, I can get into more detail if needed."

Know what I want:
- Window-washing business

↓

Ask:
"I am asking you to hire me to wash your windows."

↓

Show: ladder + bucket

↓

Best Reasons

1. I'll do a quality job on a tough chore
2. You won't have to get up on this ladder
3. I'll have it done before the holiday weekend

↓

Stop Talking

↓

Share

1. I have great referrals
2. I'm thorough
3. I guarantee your satisfaction

1. Most ER visits caused by falls from ladders
2. I only use professional grade equipment
3. I'm fully bonded

1. I can start today
2. I'll be done in 4 hours
3. I don't subcontract

"The more I look at this," I observed, rubbing my chin, "the more it looks like a script you could use when selling your services."

Warren nodded, looked at me, and said, "Like I said before, I like to keep things simple. For me the power of the Asking Formula is it's just what it says: a formula. It's logical, and it's repeatable. I use it consistently. I don't need to read a huge training manual to understand it. It's intuitive. It requires discipline, but you can use it every single day to generate success."

With that, Warren recited what he had written:

"I am asking you to hire me to wash your windows. There are many reasons for this, but three come to mind.

"First, you said you'd rather be golfing on such a fine day than washing windows. I'll do a top-notch job on a tough and messy chore.

"Second, you're not a big fan of heights; I'll get this job done, and you won't even have to get up on a ladder.

"And, finally, you want to have this job done by the Fourth of July. I'll have them sparkling before the end of day today.

"That's why I am asking to wash your windows."

I looked at him slightly awed, and Warren smiled.

Yes, not a bad script.

Warren gathered up his buckets and sponges and headed around to the back of the house. I took another look at the disturbingly untouched pile of work on my patio table and decided that I'd rather go back to selling candy door-to-door.

I found Abby listening to music in her room.

"Time for round two, Abby," I said with forced enthusiasm. "What do you say we head over to Maple Street and sell the rest of this candy?"

"Do we have to, Dad? I'm tired of selling candy."

Nothing will torpedo a girl's gumption like a dose of door-to-door rejection.

"I tell you what, Abby: we'll go out for a while and see how it goes. But this time, we'll use our 'Secret Asking Formula.' It'll make selling candy a lot easier."

This brought a spark of interest to her eyes, and she set down her iPod.

"What's our 'Secret Asking Formula'?" she asked.

"Well, I'll tell you, but you have to swear not to tell anybody else. Come over here," I said moving to her desk, "and I'll show you."

I sat at Abby's desk and opened her notebook. Abby stood and watched over my shoulder.

"OK," I stage-whispered, "the first part of the Secret Asking Formula is for you to tell me what you want."

"Not to sell candy," she said.

"OK, got it. But, we are going to go door-to-door to sell candy. So, knowing that, what do you want?"

She thought about this for a moment and said, "I want to sell all the boxes of candy in the shortest time."

"Brilliant," I shouted and wrote this down on the paper. "Now if that's what you want, how are you going to ask the person who answers the door for what you want?"

"I'll just ask, 'Would you buy all the boxes of candy?'"

Kids.

"Not bad," I said, sitting back and showing her that I was seriously pondering her answer. "But buying all the boxes of candy might be asking a lot. How about we ask the person to buy just one box?"

"OK," Abby said, shrugging and looking longingly at her iPod. On the notebook paper I wrote:

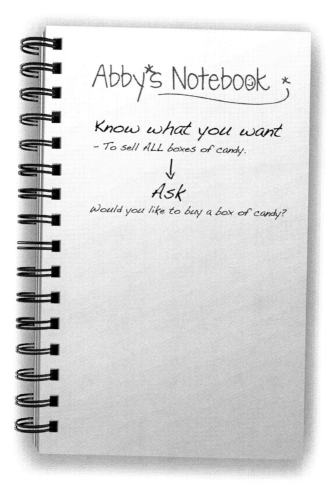

"We're halfway to the Secret Asking Formula, Abby, so pay close attention. Now, tell me all the reasons why you think someone would want to buy a box of candy from you."

"Because they have a lot of money, and I won't have to go to so many houses, and I can tell the coach that I sold all the candy and get to play in the game."

"Now, those sound like good reasons," I admitted, "but they're all reasons you have for people to buy a box of candy. We have to think of reasons they want to buy a box of candy from you."

I waited a moment to see whether Abby was following. "Try thinking about it from their perspective. Perspective is like a window: you look in from one side of the glass, but they look out from the other side. You're both looking through the same window but seeing different things. Try to see the reasons someone would have for buying a box of candy from his or her side of the glass."

Abby scrunched up her lips and gave this some thought.

"Candy tastes good," she said finally. "You can pick a box of chocolates, or caramels, or the ones with mint."

"All right, good," I said, jotting her responses down on a blank piece of paper. "What else?"

"It doesn't cost too much money. People may need to buy a present, and they won't have to go to the store to buy it."

I wrote all these down.

She paused, out of ideas.

"I think there is one more really good reason they may want to buy a box of candy," I said. "Who gets the money?"

"All the money for the candy goes to the soccer league," Abby said. "They're going to buy new nets."

"Great," I said, writing this down.

Here is what Abby's list looked like.

"We're really close to having our Secret Asking Formula," I said excitedly, "but we have to choose, out of all these reasons, the three best reasons why people will want to buy candy from you.

"For short, we'll call these our 'BRs,'" I added. "Pick one reason on the list and circle it."

Abby circled "Tastes great."

"Hard to argue with that," I said. "Now, it's my turn."

I circled "All money goes to buy new soccer nets."

"You get the last circle, Abby."

She considered the list for a while and then circled "Variety of flavors—chocolate, caramel, and mint."

"Great, we've created our Secret Asking Formula. This formula is going to make selling boxes of candy as easy as pie."

Abby looked at me questioningly. "What 'Secret Asking Formula'?"

"It's right here, Abby, exactly what we've written down: 'I am asking you to buy a box of candy that tastes great. I have a variety to choose from, and all the money goes to help the soccer league buy new nets for the city park.'"

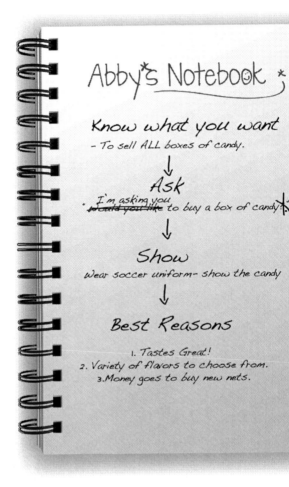

Abby's Notebook

Know what you want
- To sell ALL boxes of candy.

↓

Ask
" I'm asking you ~~would you like~~ to buy a box of candy."

↓

Show
Wear soccer uniform- show the candy

↓

Best Reasons

1. Tastes Great!
2. Variety of flavors to choose from.
3. Money goes to buy new nets.

"That's our 'Secret Asking Formula'?" she asked hesitantly.

"Trust me, Abby. If you go up to a door, ring the doorbell, and use this as your Secret Asking Formula, you'll sell all the boxes of candy in no time."

Abby is a trusting soul, but I could see she had her doubts.

"Let's practice it a few times," I said, "and then we'll test it out to see how it works."

I had Abby practice her Secret Asking Formula a few times, making it fun by emphasizing some words with silly tones. Instead of saying that the candy "tastes great," Abby would say, "It's *dee-licious*," really stretching out the word. I had her go out into the hallway and knock on her own bedroom door. Then I would open the door with a goofy grin or a sour sneer and Abby would say the Secret Asking Formula to me, laughing each time. Soon enough she became very comfortable and confident in making her pitch.

"It's show time," I said to Abby. "Let's get over to Maple Street before someone beats us there. Before we go, I want you to change into your soccer jersey so people can see that you're on a soccer team. Let's open up a box of candy, too, as a sample. That way people can see the candy, not just the box."

Abby was into it now and reenergized. She quickly changed into her jersey. I had her try the Secret Asking Formula on me once again. She looked and sounded great: who wouldn't buy a box of candy from the kid?

As we were leaving through the front door, I saw Warren out by his truck.

"Abby," I whispered out the corner of my mouth, "go test the Secret Asking Formula on Warren. Let's see whether it works."

Abby didn't hesitate. She marched over to Warren and said, "Hello, Warren. I am asking you to buy a box of candy. It's *dee-licious*. I have a lot of variety for you to choose from, and all the money goes to help buy new soccer nets at the city park." As she was saying this, Abby held up the opened box of candy so Warren could see the candy inside.

Warren froze in his tracks, and a small smile came over his lips.

"That's sounds good," he said, nodding his head. "Matter of fact, I'm in the mood for something '*dee-licious*.' I'll take a box. Do you have any caramels?"

Abby beamed and said, "Sure do!"

She fished Warren a box of caramels out of the carton and collected the money.

"Thank you, Warren! Enjoy your candy," she said.

Abby ran back over to me.

"Dad, our Secret Asking Formula works! Warren bought a box of caramels. Let's get going." With that, Abby practically ran the block over to Maple Street.

I was hoping for better results than we had experienced in our earlier effort, but the results on Maple Street were surprising even to me. Nearly eight out of every ten doors Abby knocked on bought at least one box of candy. We sold the rest of Abby's candy in less than an hour: the Secret Asking Formula worked indeed.

We walked back to the house, with Abby smiling the whole way.

"That was so easy, Dad! Thanks for helping me with the Secret Asking Formula."

She was thrilled to be able to go back to her team with her full share of the fund-raising money. I, on the other hand, was getting a slow ache in my stomach. With each step the feeling got worse.

Back at home I made Abby her favorite sandwich for lunch: fried peanut butter and banana. Then I went back out to the patio. Feeling queasy, I dug down through the untouched stack of work I had brought home from the office. Resting about halfway down was the sales presentation my company had made to McNeal Hotels. My queasiness turned into a categorically full-blown gut ache.

I paged through the presentation and saw graphs, numbers, metrics, and charts: good information my team had spent weeks preparing. We had sweated every detail, had gotten everything just right. I read the sales presentation from beginning to end and then read it again.

Not once had we asked McNeal Hotels for its business.

We had started with facts: our leading market share, our brand's stellar reputation, our new technology platform, our current inventory, delivery schedules, pricing levels, and product line specs. And, we had never asked for what we wanted.

With a sinking feeling I recalled how the audience had gotten progressively less engaged as our presentation had droned on. We had communicated from bottom to top. We had used outside-in reasons. We didn't give three Best Reasons: we gave dozens. And worst of all, most of them were from our side of the glass.

Warren was walking by and noticed my pale demeanor. "You OK?" he asked. "You look like you ate a bad egg."

"No, I am not OK," I replied. "I have come to the conclusion—in the past fifteen minutes, as a matter of fact—that my daughter who has yet to graduate from middle school knows more about being a successful salesperson than I do."

I disgustedly threw the sales presentation down onto the table.

"Warren, why is the Asking Formula such a secret? How come we don't naturally practice top-to-bottom thinking and ask for what we want first?"

Warren scratched behind his ear.

"Well, personally, I think it's fair to blame that Sherlock Holmes fella," he replied.

"Who?" I groaned.

"That guy who made 'deductive reasoning' so popular. He could deduce, simply through the power of his observation, whether someone had committed a crime, without ever having to ask a question."

"Great," I thought to myself, "I wrote a sales presentation titled 'Sherlock Holmes and the McNeal Hotels Mystery.'"

"I don't know who's to blame," Warren said with a shrug. "People are better off to ask for what they want rather than assume someone will deduce it."

When I woke up that morning, I would not have remotely understood what Warren had just said, but now it seemed so logical.

Now I knew the Asking Formula. I had seen it work. I also had seen where we had gone wrong on the McNeal Hotels account. We had left clues—facts and information—for the McNeal people to figure out. We hadn't asked for what we wanted. We hadn't given them three reasons they *would have for wanting to give us what we wanted.* They couldn't—or, more likely, didn't want to—follow the trail of clues we had left for them.

Warren began pulling little white booties over his work shoes.

"Time to do the inside windows," he said, noticing me staring at him. "Keeps me from tracking footprints on your carpet."

"Warren, I was very impressed by Abby's success using the Asking Formula," I said, pointing at the diagram on the patio window. "She wanted to sell all of her candy, and I'm convinced using that top-to-bottom approach got the job done. I wish I would have known about it earlier. It might have helped me win an account I was working on."

"Getting what you want is certainly the main benefit of the Asking Formula," Warren said. "But you'll find that the formula saves you a lot of time as well."

"I think I know how the formula saves time, Warren. You use only three BRs and three facts to back up each BR. You eliminate a lot of up-front preparation."

"I have to disagree with you there," Warren said. "The Asking Formula requires more up-front preparation, not less.

"Where it saves time," he continued, "is you know what you want and are focused on asking for it. You're less likely to stray off the agenda. Since you've done your homework, you don't get as many objections or trivial disagreements. And, the best news of all is that you get an answer right away. A yes or a no. The biggest waste of time in the world is the word 'maybe.'"

Warren moved to the patio window again. It was the only outside window that he hadn't yet washed. On it he drew the following:

Warren stood back and looked at the window. "I've had it happen where I ask and get an immediate 'Yes!' Now, that doesn't happen a whole lot, but when it does, I saved a ton of time and energy.

"Think about Abby's experience," he continued. "My guess is you had the sale pretty much right off the bat: who could say no to that girl? When you start with information, you're going the opposite direction of the Asking Formula. You're going bottom to top. You swim upstream. That takes a long time and a lot of energy."

"I agree," I said. "It infuriates me when I have to interpret what someone is trying to say to me. I just want to shout, 'Enough already! Get to the point!'"

"It's easy to bury the 'ask' with information overload," Warren said, nodding. "It can become a bad habit. Your tendency is to loop through more and more information. When you ask for something you want by looping through information, you're what I call a 'Bad Ask,'" Warren said with a sheepish grin. "You're a 'Bad Ask,'" he said again in case I missed his humor the first time.

I thought back again to the McNeal Hotels presentation: I had buried the "ask." I had practiced information looping. I . . . was . . . a . . . Bad Ask.

My son, Zack, came back out to the patio and interrupted my thoughts. Warren excused himself and went inside to his windows.

"Still no word from Elizabeth?" I asked.

"No, so I'm just going to forget the whole idea about asking her out," he said.

"Hold on now, son. Let's not call it quits so fast. How about I help you out with a formula to ask Elizabeth out on a date?"

Zack shot me a look that clearly communicated what he thought of that idea: three miles beyond inconceivable.

"What do you have to lose?" I said with a shrug. "If you don't like what I show you, you don't have to use it."

Reluctantly, he agreed. We sat at the patio table.

"Zack, what do you want?" I began.

"What do you mean?" he asked, already exasperated and at the end of his rope.

"Why are you trying to get a hold of Elizabeth?" I replied.

"To take her to the movies this coming Friday," he said.

I wrote his response down on the top of a piece of paper.

"Great, so if you want to take Elizabeth out, how would you ask her?"

"C'mon, Dad," Zack retorted, throwing up his hands. "I'd just say, y'know, 'Hey, Elizabeth, do you want to hang out on Friday?'"

"That's what you would say?" I asked, astonished.

"Oh, forget about it, Dad; you don't understand how it is with dating these days. Lots of things have changed since you were my age."

He got up to leave, but I touched his arm and motioned for him to sit back down.

"Listen: I know that the earth has cooled since I was on the dating scene, but one thing hasn't changed since I was your age: it's not easy talking to girls. But, honestly, if you ask her to 'hang out,' how do you expect her to know what you want? Do you want to change the oil in the car? Do you want to share makeup secrets? Do you want to walk around like zombies down Elm Street? What do you want?"

"I want to go on a date with her, but I can't just come out and say that," he replied.

"Why not?" I asked. "It's what you want. How are you going to get what you want if you don't ask for it?"

That got to him. I could see that he wanted to argue with me, but even for a teenager the logic was too strong to debate.

"So what would you ask for in order to get what you want?" I asked him again.

Reluctantly, he said, "Elizabeth, would you go out with me this Friday?"

I wrote this down on the notebook paper:

Know what you want:
- Take Elizabeth to the movies

Ask: "I am asking you to go out with me to the movies with me this friday."

"Great," I said. "Now give me some reasons that Elizabeth would have for giving you what you want."

"What do you mean by that?" he asked.

"Why would Elizabeth want to go on a date with you? Why Friday? Why on a real date and not just 'hanging out'? Why with just you and not with a group of kids?"

Zack thought about this for a while.

"I don't know whether Elizabeth *does* want to go out with me. She's great looking and really popular. That's the problem. But, there's a new Will Ferrell movie showing at the mall this Friday, and I think she would enjoy it. At school Elizabeth and I were talking about how much we liked his *Saturday Night Live* skits and all the movies he's made. She said her favorite movies are all comedies. We laughed a lot when we were talking, and I thought she had a great sense of humor."

I wrote all of this down.

"What else?"

"I know that it is really important that she be home by curfew, but I thought after the movie we'd still have time to share an ice cream sundae and get to know each other outside of school. She mentioned that she's sorry we don't get more time to talk during the day."

I wrote this down. "What else?"

"I'm handsome and witty," he deadpanned.

"That you are," I said, writing it down. "Just like your old man."

I looked at the list.

"I think this will do it, Zack."

Here is what we had. I shoved the list across the table to him.

Best Reasons
Why Elizabeth would want to go out with Zack:

- Elizabeth is popular

- Elizabeth is good-looking

- She likes comedy movies

- Fan of Will Ferrell

- Likes to laugh/good sense of humor

- Zack can have her home by curfew

- Wants to know Zack better

- Zack is handsome and witty

"Knowing Elizabeth, do you think these are reasons she would want to go out on a date with you to the movies?"

Zack looked at the list and nodded his assent. "I guess so," he replied.

"Good. From Elizabeth's perspective, which three of these reasons do you think are the best reasons she would have to go out on a date with you? You can circle only three."

Zack looked at the list and made a dramatic move as if to circle "Zack is handsome and witty," but instead he crossed it off the list. Then he crossed out "Elizabeth is pretty" and "Elizabeth is popular."

"She wouldn't want to go out on a date with me just because she's pretty and popular," he observed under his breath. "That's why I want to go out with her."

He kept whittling his way to three BRs, and when he was done, his list looked like this:

Best Reasons

Why Elizabeth would want to go out with Zack:

~~- Elizabeth is popular~~

~~- Elizabeth is good-looking~~

~~- She likes comedy movies~~

- Fan of Will Ferrell → SAME

#1 - Likes to laugh/good sense of humor

#2 - Zack can have her home by curfew

#3 - Wants to know Zack better

~~- Zack is handsome and witty~~

"Super," I said. I scribbled his three BRs on Zack's Asking Formula.

Know what you want:
- Take Elizabeth to the movies
↓
Ask: "I am asking you to go out ~~with me~~ to the movies with me this Friday."

Show: ↓

Best Reasons
↙ ↓ ↘

1. See a Will Ferrell movie & laugh

2. Chance to talk and get to know each other better

3. Home by curfew... guaranteed!

"I tell you what, Zack: I'm going to go check on Abby. While I'm in the house, I want you to list three facts below each one of these reasons. For example, how do you know she's a fan of Will Ferrell? How do you know you can get her home by curfew? I need three facts for each of your three Best Reasons."

I went in the house and checked on Abby, who was back listening to her iPod and dancing around her bedroom. I walked into the kitchen and saw Warren busy washing the windows over the sink.

I went back outside and found Zack finishing up his assignment. His Asking Formula now looked like this:

Know what you want:
- Take Elizabeth to the movies

↓

Ask: " I am asking you to go out ~~with me~~ to the movies with me this Friday."

Show: ↓

Best Reasons

↙   ↓   ↘

1. See a Will Ferrell movie & laugh

2. Chance to talk and get to know each other better

3. Home by curfew... guaranteed!

↓

STOP Talking

← Share →

↓

- You said you really liked his movies
- The movie has great reviews
- We laugh a lot at school

- We'll have ice cream after the movie
- It will be just you and me out on the date
- You said you'd like more time to talk

- We'll be at the local mall (3 miles away)
- I'll have you home before midnight
- We'll go to the early movie

"Zackie, my boy, this is it. You've just completed a surefire way to ask Elizabeth out on a date. This here," I said, pointing to the piece of paper in front of him, "is your Asking Formula."

Zack looked at the paper.

"Huh?"

"It's right in front of you, Zack. Look at what you have done. You've scripted a totally wonderful way to ask Elizabeth out on a date. You know what you want. You're asking for it. It's clear, and it's to the point. You've looked at the situation from her perspective." I highlighted his Asking Formula with a yellow marker. "Just read what you've written."

Zack picked up the piece of paper and began reading:

"Elizabeth, I am asking you to go out to the movies with me this Friday. We can see the new Will Ferrell movie and have some laughs. We'd have a chance to get to know one another better. And, I guarantee I'll have you home by curfew."

I whistled. "Zack, that was fantastic."

He read it out loud again. Then again. Then one more time.

"Hey, this is pretty neat," he said, looking at me with surprise. "It's exactly what I want to say."

"Exactly," I said. "And my guess is that if you ask politely and confidently, Elizabeth won't be able to resist saying yes."

"But what if she says no?" Zack asked, clearly worried about the prospect.

"Then you have your answer," I replied with a shrug. "Listen: there aren't any guarantees. You may not like her answer. But at least you'll feel that you asked her the best way you could."

"Yeah, I guess you're right," Zack said. He took a big breath and let the air out slowly. "Well, there's no time like the present. I'm going to give her a call and see what she has to say."

He reached into his pocket and came out with his cell phone. He looked at me, put his phone back in his pocket, and got up from the table.

"No offense, Dad, but I want to do this in private." He turned and went into the house.

"Good luck," I called after him.

I breathed deeply. The McNeal presentation book lay splayed open where I had tossed it in disgust.

The Asking Formula had worked selling candy door-to-door. It provided the confidence for a teenaged boy to ask a girl out on a date. It produced a model for a window washer to grow his business.

Could it have made the difference in the McNeal presentation?

Before I could ponder this question any deeper, I saw my neighbor Larry walking over from across the street. Larry was a great guy, and despite the fact that he was inclined to borrow my tools without returning them, I couldn't ask for a better neighbor.

Recently, Larry had been struggling with finding a new job. He had been let go about seven months ago from a CFO position at a midsized manufacturer. Larry had been an innocent downsizing victim of a corporate decision to relocate certain operations to an offshore vendor.

Larry had interviewed for several new positions but never quite made it far enough in the process to get the offer. He had come in second a couple of times, which was frustrating. As his job search dragged on, the stress he felt was beginning to show. He kept on a brave face, but I could tell that sitting idle for over half of a year, for a talented and ambitious guy like Larry, was driving him crazy.

"Hi, neighbor," he greeted me. He held up a box of chocolates. "A nice young lady sold this candy to me earlier today, and I thought you might like a piece."

I laughed and shook my head. "I'm OK on candy, so no thanks. But have a seat. Want some lemonade?"

Larry shook his head at my offer of lemonade, sat down, and did a once-over on my table full of work.

"Looks like you brought more work home," he commented. "Glad things are busy. You know, I wouldn't mind doing some weekend work. This unemployment is tough."

"What's new on the job search front?" I asked.

Larry let out a big sigh. "Good and bad. I've gotten a lot of interest in my résumé but haven't hit pay dirt yet. I'm still trying to get over coming in second on that Rippen Corporation search. That was a killer. I thought I was the perfect candidate and was sure I was going to get an offer. I probably interviewed for the position with no fewer than six different people over the past three months."

"Did Rippen give you any reason why it chose someone else?" I asked.

"You know how these debriefs go," Larry sighed again. "The people there said that it had been a very tough call. That they were convinced both final candidates could do the job and ultimately it came down to a style fit. Hard to know whether they're being fully honest, but that's what they said."

Larry slouched back in the chair and looked over at his house.

"The good news is that I'm one of the finalists for a CFO position at Becker Manufacturing. I have an interview with the CEO on Wednesday. Unfortunately, I think it's going to come down to me and one other guy again. After the Rippen deal fell through, I don't want to get my hopes up too much."

A siren went off in my head. If Larry held back his enthusiasm about the Becker Manufacturing job because he feared that he would get another "no," it seemed logical that he'd come off as less than enthusiastic to the Becker people about his desire for the job. It was a self-defeating attitude. I glanced up at the Asking Formula on my patio window.

"Larry," I asked, "when you interviewed at Rippen, did you ask for the job?"

He was taken aback by my question. "What do you mean?"

I scratched my head and said, "If you were one of two final candidates who were equally qualified for the job, I'm wondering whether the deciding factor was who asked for the job and who didn't."

"Well, after three months of interviews," Larry said defensively, "I would hope that someone there would have figured out I wanted the job."

"But, did you ask for it?" I persisted.

Larry thought about this for a good while. "No," he finally said, "I guess I never did. I'm not sure that it would have mattered."

"I'm not sure, either," I admitted, "but it may be one thing you can learn from your Rippen experience and do differently with the opportunity at Becker Manufacturing. You said you're meeting with the CEO on Wednesday; there might not be a better time for you to ask for the job than during that meeting."

Larry looked puzzled, frustrated, and doubtful all at once. Finally, he nodded his head and said, "Why not? If asking for the job is the thing that gets me over the hump, I'm all for it. During my interview with the CEO next week, I'll make a point to ask for the job."

"Good," I said reassuringly. "For what it's worth, I think it's important. And, it certainly can't hurt anything. How are you going to ask?"

"I hadn't thought about it," Larry replied nonchalantly. "I guess I'll say that my background and experience are perfect for the job and I hope to be seriously considered for the position."

Maybe it could hurt, I thought to myself. If Larry asked like that, he would come off as unenthusiastic, unprepared, and unqualified. I glanced at the Asking Formula sketched on my patio window again.

"Let me ask you this, Larry: what do you want from the CEO at Becker Manufacturing?"

"What do I want?" Larry asked.

"What do you want as a result of the meeting?" I asked again.

"Well," Larry said indecisively, "I want to be considered a quality candidate. I want the CEO to be impressed with my résumé. I don't want to blow the chance to be—"

"Larry," I interrupted, "what do you want?"

Larry stopped talking.

After a long pause, he said, "I want the job, dammit I want to be hired."

I took a piece of paper from my folder and wrote this down.

"That's what I thought," I said. "Now how are you going to ask for it?"

"Ask for the job?" Larry said, acting surprised.

"Yes, Larry, you just told me that is what you want. Role-play with me. Pretend it's Wednesday and I'm the CEO. How are you going to ask for what you want?"

Larry collected his thoughts and then began speaking: "I appreciate the opportunity to interview with Becker Manufacturing. As you can see by my résumé, I have an extensive background in finance. I am a licensed CPA with experience as a CFO in a midsized manufacturer. During my most recent position I held dual roles as CFO and corporate treasurer. I introduced new manufacturing disciplines that saved the company over . . ."

I let Larry continue for about two more minutes. He was practicing what Warren had called looping behavior. He was being a Bad Ask: leading with information, not asking for what he wanted. He was cycling through things the CEO could easily discern from his résumé. If I had been the actual CEO, I would have stopped listening.

I held up my hand to indicate that I wanted him to stop talking.

"Larry, what do you want?"

He caught himself midsentence. "You're right," he acknowledged. "I haven't gotten around to what I want to ask for yet. I guess I feel the need to brag myself up a bit before I cut to the chase."

"Everything you just told me," I observed, "I already know about you. You're not asking for what you want as much as reading me your résumé.

"Try it again," I urged. "But, this time, get to the point right away."

Larry collected his thoughts and started anew: "Thank you for the opportunity to interview with Becker Manufacturing. I am asking you to consider me as the primary candidate for this position, and I would like a job offer."

Larry stopped.

"That sounds so . . . so . . . forward," he said.

"No, it didn't, Larry," I replied with a big grin. "To me it sounded like you know exactly what you want and are confident enough to ask for it."

"Really?" he asked. "It doesn't make me sound too brazen?"

"Far from it," I exclaimed. "Listen: I'm the CEO. I'm busy. I want people to be direct and straightforward with me. I don't have time to beat around the bush. Get to the point. I appreciate it."

Larry nodded. I could see that he was becoming convinced of the power of the Asking Formula.

"Now, finish your ask, Larry," I encouraged him. "Why should I want to give you the job?"

"Why should you want to give me the job?" he muttered to himself. After thinking for a moment he said, "I'm highly qualified."

"So is the other guy," I immediately replied.

"I've been a successful CFO at a similar firm and done similar work," he said.

"So has the other guy," I replied again.

He paused and said, "I'm really excited about the opportunity."

"So were all the other candidates," I said flatly. "Why should I want to give *you* the job?"

I could see he was getting frustrated.

"Larry," I asked in a calming voice, "how long have you been interviewing with Becker? How many folks have you interviewed with?"

"It's been another one of those drawn-out processes," he answered. "My first interview was four months ago, and I bet I've talked to no fewer than eight people."

"OK," I replied. "During all that time, meeting with all those people, did you hear any of them discuss a specific need they have? Or a particular pain point causing them headaches? The reason I want to give you what you want—which you just said is to make you a job offer—is that you can solve my problems. When you ask for what you want, remind me of my problems and tell me how you can solve them."

Larry nodded. "I get it," he said. "Becker has all kinds of inventory control problems. In fact, I think the incumbent CFO was let go because he couldn't get a handle on the carrying costs. I bring special experience to these types of problems. In my last job I shortened our product delivery cycle by nearly four weeks and reduced inventory costs by half. In fact, I was given a Prestige Award for my work by the Association of Inventory Management."

Without him knowing what to call it, I could see Larry knew that he had just nailed a Best Reason.

"Whoa," I said. "As your future CEO, I'm interested. That's good stuff. Now, tell me two more things that you want to solve for me."

Larry continued: "From what I've learned, Becker also has very lax project management procedures. I can't tell whether the investment spending is efficient, but I know it's a big item in the company's budget. In fact, it's going through an expensive system conversion and spending millions on new hardware and software. I can immediately put into place project management disciplines that ensure Becker squeezes every dollar out of its investment spend."

"That's very impressive," I noted. "As CEO I need to know my capital is being spent in the most efficient way possible. Now, tell me one more thing you're going to do for me."

Larry stirred in his seat. He was gaining energy and motivation.

"Well," he said, "this might be a bit different from the first two reasons, but every time I talked with someone at Becker, I came away from the interaction feeling that everyone there is very culture conscious. I think the ex-CFO was a really difficult person to deal with. People kept telling me that the role of CFO at Becker is to help grow the business, not just push the numbers. I got a real sense that they want a team player. I know they want someone who is good at crunching data, but they also want someone who can add value to sales and marketing."

"OK," I said, "what does that mean to me?"

"In my past role," Larry continued, "I initiated a cross-organizational committee that looked at strategies to increase our market share. Because we brought everyone's expertise to bear on the issue, we were able to grow and take business from our competition. And, it was a heck of a lot of fun."

"So, you're a finance guy, but you know how to grow market share," I stated. "That's a rare combination. I like the energy you had when you gave me that example. I can tell it was something you enjoyed."

I paused for a second. "Now, Larry, finish your ask. Start as you did before and ask directly for what you want. But, this time, tell me the three Best Reasons you think I should give you what you want."

I noticed Larry's body language had changed from passive and compliant to engaged and energized. He asked for a piece of paper and spent a couple of minutes jotting down his thoughts.

"OK, here goes," he said. "Thank you for the opportunity to interview with Becker Group Manufacturing. I am asking you to consider me as the primary candidate for this position, and I would like a job offer.

"There are many great reasons for this, but three reasons jump out at me.

"First, by talking with your people, I know you're very concerned about your current inventory controls. I literally wrote the white paper on this issue, and my case studies on the subject have appeared in the industry's leading journals. No one else can hit this issue with the level of thought leadership the way I can. We'll have controls in place that will not only reduce your carrying cost but also shorten product delivery lead times.

"Second, I know you have concerns with your current investment spending levels. I read in your latest letter to shareholders that this is a strategic focus for you in the coming year. I can immediately implement best-practice methodologies that will identify areas of waste as well as uncover opportunities for leverage. My past experience demonstrates that I can deliver productivity improvements in the 25% to 50% range.

"Finally, I can pick up a real esprit de corps in your organization. In fact, from my conversations with members of your team, I can tell that working together is a high priority. I work best in a collaborative environment. My efforts to break down organizational silos have been highly recognized and highly productive. I'm a finance guy who can nail the numbers but also enjoys working outside the box in nontraditional initiatives."

Larry stopped. I sat back in my chair and began to applaud. Larry feigned an "Aw, shucks" expression.

"It was nothing," he said, doing fake bow.

Call it an omen, a celestial sign, or just serendipity, but at that very moment the sun emerged from behind a cloud. Larry and I both laughed at the coincidence.

"Larry, that was far from nothing," I countered. "That was masterful. You nailed it. Without knowing any more details about Becker Manufacturing, I can tell that you really took the time to understand the business and that you're focused on solving its problems. Your 'ask' was marvelous. Well done."

"This truly is a remarkable process," Larry said with a slight shake of his head. "I never would have thought that asking for what I want could be so directly tied to my success. I can't say for sure that this will get me the job, but I can tell you I feel infinitely more confident than when I first sat down at this table. This has been really helpful. What can I do to repay you?"

I chuckled to myself. Repay me? How about repaying Warren for his window-washing wisdom?

"There is one thing you can do, Larry," I said with mock gravity in my voice. "You can return my power drill. I need it this weekend, you've had it for a month, and you said you needed it only for a small project you were working on."

Without missing a beat Larry shouted, "Consider it done!"

He stretched out his hand, and I shook it. "Seriously, I can't tell you how thankful I am," he said.

Larry's whole demeanor had changed. When he had walked over, he looked downtrodden and defeated. On his way back across the street, he walked with confidence and purpose. He was a man who knew how to ask for what he wanted. The Asking Formula had worked its magic again.

Warren walked by carrying his ladder and bucket.

"Well, I'm done," he said. "Everything is sparkling clean except for this patio window." He tilted his head at the window with the Asking Formula diagram still drawn on it with soapy streaks. "It'll take me just a minute to wash it and I'll be on my way."

I looked at the window and then back at Warren. "That's OK," I said. "Leave it. I want to think about what we've talked about today. The Asking Formula. I'll wash the window when I'm done."

"Fair enough," said Warren with a small grin. With that, he loaded up his van, waved good-bye, and drove off to his next client.

Alone now on the patio, I once again looked at the McNeal presentation. Could the Asking Formula have won the McNeal Hotels account?

My firm had hoped to take over the servicing for all of McNeal's employee benefits programs. McNeal had been using five different vendors to provide what we could do in one package. But consolidating all its services to one vendor was new thinking for McNeal, and to achieve our objective, we needed to convince the company not only that we could do the job but also that we would be better at servicing each component of the benefits program than the incumbents.

I took out a piece of paper.

Know *what I want:* — *Win the McNeal Hotels account*

↓

Ask: *"I am asking this committee to select my company as your service provider for all your employee benefit plans."*

On another piece of paper I wrote reasons I felt McNeal would want to give me what I wanted.

I had done a lot of research on McNeal Hotels in preparation for our initial presentation, but for this exercise I focused exclusively on the reasons that would most resonate with a company of its size and complexity. In addition, I concentrated on the reasons that wouldn't lead McNeal to an alternative decision, such as choosing us for one part of the servicing and not the whole package.

Here is the list I wrote:

Best Reasons

Why McNeal would want to give us their business?

- Each of our service components is rated the highest in client satisfaction.

- Industry trends shifting to 1 vendor model.

- Invested > $50mm in new technology.

- Capacity to convert business asap.

- Industry leader in handling multiple locations.

- Consolidated information enables employees to call 1 phone # for their needs and questions.

- Net costs for services are lower.

- History of keeping fees from rising.

- Offer a money back guarantee

I wanted to make sure my BRs were indisputable, so I took the time to lay out each and examine it under the facts I knew about McNeal, its culture, and the constitution of the team it had chartered to make the purchase decision.

On a piece of notebook paper I put together this matrix:

Reason	Best Reason?	Rationale
Service rated on each component	Yes #3	McNeal wants absolute assurance that we can handle the whole service portfolio as well as or even better than the individual vendors currently doing the work
Industry Trends	No	Who cares? McNeal prides itself on not following the crowd. Following trends doesn't make them tick nor is it in their culture
$50mm in Tech investment	No	Appeals to the tech representative on the McNeal team but she is not ultimate decision maker
Convert ASAP	No	Never mentioned as a priority by McNeal
Leader in multiple locations	Yes #2	McNeal has 1,400 locations across North America and is growing every year
1 Phone # for employee calls	Yes #1	McNeal's CEO, the key decision maker, expressed "helping employees" as a number one corporate objective
Lower Costs	No	Bad conclusion of Asking Formula, leads McNeal into a comparison that focuses on costs
Fee Stability	No	So What?
Money back guarantee	No	A bad decision by McNeal would be so costly that a fee refund would be insignificant

This work led me to the following:

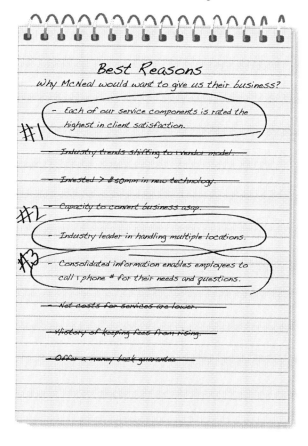

Best Reasons

Why McNeal would want to give us their business?

#1 - Each of our service components is rated the highest in client satisfaction.

~~Industry trends shifting to vendor model.~~

~~Invested > $50mm in new technology.~~

#2 ~~Capacity to convert business asap.~~

- Industry leader in handling multiple locations.

#3 - Consolidated information enables employees to call 1 phone # for their needs and questions.

~~Net costs for services are lower.~~

~~History of keeping fees from rising.~~

~~Offer a money-back guarantee.~~

I was now ready for my Asking Formula:

Know what I want: — Win the McNeal Hotels account

↓

Ask: "I am asking this committee to select my company as your service provider for all your employee benefit plans."

↓

Show: Happy McNeal employees

↓ **Best Reasons**

1. McNeal's Employees will have 1 phone # for all their needs

2. Highly experienced in dealing with multiple locations

3. Each of our service components is best in class.

The underlining facts would be the easiest part: our original presentation had more than forty slides' worth of information and facts. The tricky part was the three-fact limit required by the Asking Formula:

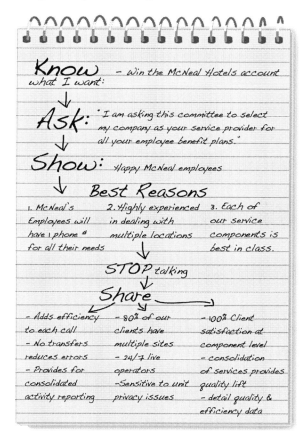

I sat back. The clarity of McNeal Hotels' Asking Formula was astounding. On one page I had synthesized a forty-slide presentation.

And, most importantly, it laid a clear path for me to ask McNeal Hotels for what I wanted.

Zack interrupted my thoughts.

"Hey, Dad, I got a hold of Elizabeth," he said, his head hanging low as he stared at the ground.

"And . . .?" I asked.

"I'm picking her up at seven o'clock on Friday to go see a movie and have some ice cream! She said she is really looking forward to it." He whooped and jumped into the air. Then he ran over to give me a high five.

I started laughing.

"Congratulations, Romeo."

Zack blushed, but he was grinning ear-to-ear.

"Thanks for the help, Dad. That stuff you taught me really works."

"No sweat, kid. I'm happy you got what you wanted."

I turned back to the Asking Formula for the McNeal Hotels account. The coherence of the page caused me to wonder: could this actually be the entire presentation? What if we limited our talking points to just this one page, put all other data into an appendix, and stuck to the flow of the diagram? I circled each stage of the diagram:

The sharpness of the conversation we could have had with the McNeal team was undeniable. In eight slides we would have made our case. In eight slides we would have addressed McNeal's hot buttons and provided crisp responses for each of its needs. Our presentation would have been airtight.

Then, I thought: how about a slide with photographs of members of my staff talking to happy McNeal Hotels employees as if they were working through some benefits questions? *Show what you're asking for.*

Would we have won the deal? Impossible to say but I knew in my gut that our chances would have been greatly enhanced. Our presentation would have stood out in the crowd: short, concise, and to the point.

Top to bottom. Inside and out. Three Best Reasons.

I was deep in concentration and startled by Zack clearing his throat.

"Say, Dad," Zack said. "I'm asking to use the car this Friday. I'll drive responsibly. I'll buy my own gas. And, I'll have it back in the garage by 12:15."

"This Friday? I don't see why . . . hey, wait one minute: you're using the Asking Formula on me!" I exclaimed.

Zack laughed out loud. "Yup. Like I said: this stuff really works."

AFTERWORD

Of course, I could never know whether using the Asking Formula would have won the McNeal Hotels account. But by using it, we subsequently won the Continental Cargo account. And Countrywide Trucking, JaCo Pharmaceutical, and Specialty Mining.

I was so impressed with what I had learned on the patio that I decided to train my entire staff on its use for all future presentations.

The results were dramatic: close ratios went up, sales cycles shortened, and the confidence of the team was dramatically enhanced. My team thought they could win every deal. We regained a momentum I thought was permanently lost. The Asking Formula is easy to learn and straightforward to use, and it became our standard way of selling business.

I also trained other areas of the company on the Asking Formula. Its use became both a corporate expectation and a part of our internal culture. No more two-hour presentations with fifty PowerPoint slides. No more endless meetings and nonstop e-mails.

Project managers ask for funding by using the Asking Formula, and line managers use the Asking Formula when making staffing requests. Our client relationship managers use the Asking Formula to structure their account reviews with our clients. It has become embedded in the way we do business.

In addition, our internal company communications became sharper. A by-product of using the Asking Formula was that people began structuring memos and e-mails in a top-to-bottom, inside-out manner.

All because of a simple conversation with a window washer.

But the story doesn't end there.

I use the Asking Formula in my personal interactions as well. Conversations with my wife are clearer and result in fewer misunderstandings. The Asking Formula is a super technique when interacting with children of all ages—especially teenagers—as it appeals to their need for logic and consistency. My kids have learned how to use the Asking Formula with their teachers, coaches, and peers.

I became less tentative when communicating difficult or uncomfortable messages. Larry even made good on his commitment to return my drill.

The Asking Formula changed my life.

I learned how to ask for what I want—and get it.

WHAT'S NEXT?

How can I put the power of the Asking Formula to work in my life?

- Generate more results and get what you want more frequently by using the Asking Formula in both your professional life and your personal life. Go to **www.theaskingformula.com** for more tools that will help you practice and reinforce the powerful message of this book.

- Have John deliver his extraordinary keynote or workshop to your team and drive the Asking Formula into daily practice.

- Engage your entire organization by bringing the Asking Formula training system to your sales team and nonsales leaders. Imagine the efficiency and effectiveness of having an entire culture built on the clarity and simplicity of the Asking Formula's design.

- Align this message with your client marketing and loyalty programs by exposing your clients to John's motivational message at an upcoming client event.

- Buy a block of books and have your team discuss how they can use the Asking Formula specifically targeted at the issues and opportunities they face.

- Present the book to someone who is facing an "asking" situation in his or her life and needs a shot of confidence to bolster his or her effectiveness.

- **Follow the Asking Formula on Facebook.** Check it out, make a comment, and get updates and tips on how to become the best "asker" possible.

For more information on the Asking Formula programs and services, please visit **www.theaskingformula.com**.

A NOTE FROM JOHN BAKER:

The feedback I have received on the Asking Formula has been, since its creation, nothing short of a phenomenon. People who have read this book, attended a workshop, or visited www.theaskingformula.com have shared their unique stories on how this program has changed their lives. Many have said that they wished they had been exposed earlier to the Asking Formula, as they can imagine the positive impact it could have made on their career and personal relationships. As Warren might say, I like to keep things simple, and, generally speaking, you don't get what you want in life unless you ask for it. So learning how to ask in the most effective way possible is a crucial skill and essential to our success.

What I want:

For you to pass the Asking Formula along to someone in your network and become an "Asking Formula Agent": someone who knows the secret of persuasive communications.

My Ask:

I am asking you to share this book and its message with those you feel can benefit.

Best Reason #1:

You've enjoyed this book's simple and straightforward message, and so will others. The Asking Formula is one of the most immediate and accessible ways to generate self-improvement.

Best Reason #2:

You have decided that the Asking Formula can make you a better, more persuasive, and confident communicator. Sharing the methodology with those in your network simply means you're interested in giving them a best practice to do the same.

Best Reason #3:

Whether it be . . .

- a sales rookie or a salty veteran,
- a newly minted manager or a CEO,
- a student or a seasoned professional,
- someone in a new relationship or a happily married couple . . .

the Asking Formula can profoundly improve the outcomes we seek in our lives.

—John